CW00430495

The JET SKI Book

The JET SKI Book

A JET SKI INTERNATIONAL GUIDE

CHRIS BOILING

FERNHURST

© Fernhurst Books 1991

First published in 1991 by Fernhurst Books, 33 Grand Parade, Brighton, East Sussex

All rights reserved. No part of this publication may be reproduced, stored in a retrieval system or transmitted in any form or by any means electronic, mechanical, photocopying, recording or otherwise, without the prior permission of the publisher.

Printed and bound in Great Britain

British Library Cataloguing in Publication Data
Boiling, Christopher
  The jet ski book.
  I. Title
  797.35

ISBN 0-906754-65-8

Acknowledgements
The author and publisher would like to thank the following riders for their help in producing this book. In Britain: Anthony Dean, Phil Wade, Roy Steemson, Tony Walker and Tim Rochfort; in the USA: Jeff Jacobs, Larry Rippenkroeger, Scott Watkins, Victor Sheldon, Sheldon Messick and Chris Fishetti; and in France: Andre Cosson and Richard Rocal. Special thanks also to Alan Hesselden and Tony Walker for their technical assistance; and to the Kawasaki Information Service, the UK Jet Ski Association and John Driscoll of the RYA for their assistance with the text.

Photographs
Most of the photographs in this book are by Chris Boiling/*Jet Ski International*. Others courtesy of Clay Jacobson, Kawasaki, Mitsui Machinery (Yamaha), Ralph Campos/Mobby's Wetsuits, Solas Impellers, Calkins Manufacturing and Wellcraft Scarab. The cover photograph is by Chris Boiling.

Every effort has been made to locate the copyright holders of all material used in this book, but the publishers disclaim all responsibility for mistakes in attribution where the copyright ownership is not made clear on the material.

Edited by Tom Willis
Designed by Joyce Chester/Jenny Searle
Composition by Central Southern Typesetters, Eastbourne
Artwork courtesy of the Kawasaki Information Service
Printed by Ebenezer Baylis & Son, Worcester

CONTENTS

1 THEN AND NOW

INTRODUCTION

Jet Ski riding is the sport of the 1990s. It gets you out in the fresh air and keeps you fit. It's fast, action-packed and, compared with other motor sports, cheap. It also boasts a remarkable safety record.

It draws on skills and offers thrills: skills from a variety of sports such as motorcycling, snowskiing, waterskiing and windsurfing, thrills from the surge of power at your fingertips. Even standard machines will give around 40mph, a speed that feels positively supersonic so close to the surface of the water.

But speed isn't everything. Ride it fast or slow, cruise, race or perform tricks – whatever you want to do, a Jet Ski makes it fun.

And if you want to compete against other enthusiasts, there is a well-organised racing and competition circuit in Britain, Europe and the United States.

WARNING

Although Jet Ski riding is a safe sport, many of the advanced techniques depicted in this book are potentially dangerous if you are not an experienced skier. Virtually all the riders in our photos are experts or professionals. Do not attempt to duplicate any stunts that are beyond your own capabilities, and always wear the appropriate safety gear.

THE HISTORY OF THE JET SKI

Thirty years ago an American motorcycle racer was sitting on the ground, picking gravel out of the cuts on his hands after a tough day's racing. Clay Jacobson liked the thrill of racing, but his body was beginning to resent the spills. "There's got to be a better way," he thought.

Eventually he hit on the idea of a powered waterski – fast, exciting, and best of all, no gravel. It would be a lot safer than biking, and less dependent on other people than skiing. It took him five years of experimenting before he got a craft on the water, and seven prototypes before he arrived at something close to today's Jet Ski.

In 1968 a Canadian manufacturer produced the world's first personal watercraft based on Jacobson's design, the Bombardier Sea-Doo. But it wasn't successful, and Jacobson went back to the drawing board.

The next prototype was built with a vee hull, a fixed handlebar assembly and a Rotax water-cooled engine. The basic idea worked, but the craft proved extremely difficult to ride and produced some amazing spills for the intrepid test riders. Nevertheless, it was a start.

Jacobson now went in search of a major manufacturer to back his project. Yamaha and Honda turned him down; Kawasaki USA saw the potential of his invention, which he called the Jet Ski, and took it on in 1971.

The aim was to make the Jet Ski portable, easy to use, affordable by a wide group of

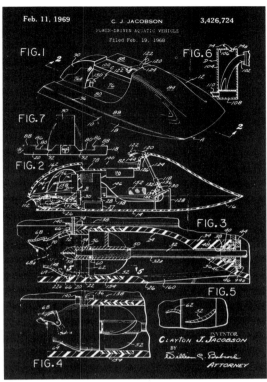

TOP Clay Jacobson with the world's second Jet Ski ABOVE The Bombardier Sea-Doo GT of 1990

Jacobson's Sea-Doo patent, filed in 1968 – the beginning of it all

buyers, and with a wide appeal to teenagers and adults alike. The first of the new series of prototypes was ready for testing in early 1972, powered by the 400cc twin-cylinder two-stroke engine used in Kawasaki's snowmobiles.

Over the next six months the prototype changed five times. The centre of gravity was lowered to make it self-righting, and the hull form continuously refined to achieve the ideal balance between cornering performance and high-speed stability. The eventual solution was a scalloped hull, with rounded grooves running the length of the hull for stability and bite on the turns. The engine bay was made watertight, the electrics waterproofed, the handlepole hinged

at the base, and as a final refinement the craft was made to circle round automatically in the event of the rider taking a tumble.

The first Jet Ski 400s, in lime green and bright yellow, went on limited test market sale in 1973. By 1975 demand had completely outstripped supply. A new production line was established in 1976 alongside snowmobiles and motorcycles at Kawasaki's factory in Lincoln, Nebraska, producing Jet Ski watercraft by the thousand.

The basic JS400 of 1976 is still in the catalogue, now renamed the JS440 and with refinements such as fingertip control and sealed electrics that have improved it beyond measure. But now it is one of a whole family of Kawasaki Jet Ski watercraft.

In 1982 Kawasaki introduced a higher-powered model, the 550. This used a new 550cc motor coupled to a large-volume pump in basically the same 440 hull, but fitted with side stabilizers to cope with the increased top speed. By 1986 even this was not enough for power-hungry Jet Ski enthusiasts, and major engine revisions were undertaken which boosted the power to 40bhp.

1986 also saw the introduction of the X-2, a 50hp two-seater, and a low-priced entry-level model made in Japan, powered by a single-cylinder two-stroke engine and called the JS300. The 650cc engine of the X-2 provided the power for the next development, the single-rider 650SX.

ABOVE The world's first Jet Ski, 1966 . . .
. . . and how it looks in the 1990s BELOW

The stage was now set for the decade. The appeal of the sport is best illustrated by one of its most successful converts, Larry Rippenkroeger, a former professional motocross rider and now two-times world Jet Ski champion:

"The first time I rode a Jet Ski, I came away thinking it was the hardest thing I'd ever tried in my life. I'd always been real athletic – I could pick things up and get fairly good at them in a fairly short period of time. But riding a Jet Ski was just the opposite. I mean, I was the worst."

He remembers his first ride well: "The guys that took me out told me as little as possible 'cause, you know, I'm this big motorcycle racer and I'm doing real well in this area and they're gonna show me. I

ABOVE *It's 1972 and a Kawasaki Jet Ski hits the water. Its number is 0000001*

RIGHT *Testing time for a 1967 prototype*

didn't even know you could ride on your knees! I mean, they just took off from the beach with one foot in the tray.

"Instruction? They said, OK, here's the start button, just pull the throttle and go. I went about 20 feet.

"Finally, I figured out myself that you could sit on your knees for a while, get the feel of it. But I came in after about half an hour just draggin', so exhausted I couldn't move.

"But I was hooked from the start. A few weeks after I first tried one, I bought a JS400 and after that I just put the motocross bikes away and sold 'em – never went out on them again." He took up speedway and the Jet Ski, enjoying great success on the

track but major problems on the water.

"Speedway? I went from Division III to Division I in a matter of weeks. Jet Skis? I was terrible. But that's why I really went after it, because it was such a challenge. I kept thinking 'I just can't figure this out.'"

Competition was quick to develop. The Northern California Jet Skiers, probably the oldest Jet Ski club in the world, hosted their first Jet Ski race in 1977. Soon there was a regular schedule of club events all over the States.

Jet Ski racing got a major boost in 1980 when Kawasaki stepped in with an offer of $10,000 purses for each of three big races. Suddenly, the sport had hit the big time.

The sport grew overseas as well as in the

US. Tony Walker, the man who first brought Kawasaki Jet Ski watercraft to Britain, recalls the early days: "For me, Jet Ski riding came to life in idyllic surroundings. I was sunbathing on a Barbados beach in 1979 when, around the headland, I spotted four guys riding what I could only describe as water scooters. They must have thought it was Christmas – there I was, running down the beach, plying them with dollars for my first 20-minute ride. Like a schoolboy with a new bike, I was hooked.

"After this first encounter I spent the next six months exchanging letters and phone calls and finally making two visits to Kawasaki's headquarters in California to gain the contract to import and distribute Jet Ski watercraft in the UK. The first machines arrived in 1980.

"I have to say that most of my business associates thought I was crazy. 'How could a water scooter sell in such a cold climate?' they asked. I tried to explain that it wasn't just a water scooter, it was a sport, but they weren't convinced. However, I was. All I had to do now was bring the rest of the nation round to my way of thinking."

Throughout the 1980s, on both sides of the Atlantic, more riders took up the challenge. More racing classes were added, and the sport gained steadily more exposure. Now, twenty-one years after Clay Jacobson teamed up with Kawasaki, the sport has finally come of age.

A Kawasaki X2 in race action

Yamaha's Jet Ski lookalike, the Super Jet

WHAT IS A JET SKI?

Jet Ski is the registered trade mark used by Kawasaki to denote their own brand of personal watercraft. There are now two-seater Jet Ski watercraft as well as solo models, but in this book we will be concentrating on the solos. These have certain common features:

A water-cooled Kawasaki engine of approximately 300, 440, 550 or 650cc;

Water jet drive – much safer than propeller drive, because there are no external blades to injure the rider;

A glassfibre hull filled with closed-cell foam buoyancy so that even if it is holed the boat will not sink;

An open-backed riding platform (or tray); and

A hinged, steerable handlepole supporting handlebars with start and stop buttons and a throttle control. Turning the handlebars turns the jet nozzle at the rear of the craft, altering the direction of flow of the water jet and making the Jet Ski turn.

There are four solo models currently in the UK line-up – the 300, 440, 550SX and 650SX – and another 300 variation in the US. There is also a growing range of Kawasaki two-seater craft, all sharing a similar 650cc twin-cylinder two-stroke power unit, and differing from the solo models in that they do not have the distinctive rising handlepole.

The most popular two-seater, the X-2, can be ridden solo either standing, kneeling or sitting on the central seat, the handlebars being locked into any of three positions to suit. Experienced Jet Ski riders can ride this machine two-up, but this is greatly simplified by adding a pair of optional pontoons. With these bolted in place, the X-2 is a very stable family craft.

The personal watercraft market is a volatile one, and a graveyard for all sorts of products that appear at shows and dealerships for a couple of years and then disappear without trace. But Bombardier, the Canadian manufacturer of Clay Jacobson's original machine, are still producing their Sea-Doo, and latecomers Yamaha have over the last five years developed a wide range of personal watercraft. Most of these are two-seaters, but there is now a Yamaha equivalent to the Jet Ski, the Super Jet, which has a 650cc engine and a hinged handlepole.

2 GETTING STARTED

BUYING A JET SKI

Undoubtedly the best way to enjoy Jet Ski riding is with your own boat. Every machine has its own performance and handling characteristics, and to get the most out of it you need to be familiar with its idiosyncrasies. Owning your own craft gives you a chance to develop that familiarity, which you'll never get if only ever hire Jet Ski watercraft and have to take out a different machine every time you ride.

Also, having your own machine means that you can choose on the spur of the moment when and where to go skiing. The good rental operations and ski clubs get very crowded on summer weekends and evenings. At the times most convenient to you it's likely that you will either have to book well in advance or travel a long way to sit around on the bank waiting for a machine to come free.

If you're in the market for a new machine, buy it from an authorised dealer, who will be able to carry out the necessary pre-delivery inspection, service it at the appropriate intervals and honour the manufacturer's warranty. Kawasaki Jet Ski watercraft are very reliable, but if something goes wrong you will want it dealt with as soon as possible, and many dealers make a policy of giving service and maintenance priority to customers who bought machines from them.

Buying secondhand is a bit more tricky, especially for someone who has never owned a personal watercraft before. Private pur-

RIGHT If you lend your ski to a friend, make sure he or she knows how to use it, and understands the safety regulations

BELOW Riding in the sea can sometimes be trickier than riding on a flat, calm lake

chase is cheaper: look in the pages of specialist magazines such as *Jet Ski International*, local papers and *Exchange & Mart*. The notice board at your local club is also a good marketplace. But you'll need to take along a knowledgeable friend to look the craft over. If you buy from a dealer, you'll pay more, but you should get a guarantee – and more peace of mind.

If you lend your craft to a friend, make sure they know the rules and how to operate the craft safely. Don't lend it to anyone you wouldn't also lend your car.

WHERE TO SKI

For the beginner, lakes are the best place to learn to Jet Ski, because the water is reasonably flat and the safety of shore is never too far away. Unfortunately, in the UK, most inland stretches of open water open to the public are subject to speed limits that effectively prevent the use of personal watercraft on them, so freshwater riders will almost certainly have to join a club.

The UK Jet Ski Association can provide a full list.

In the US, the situation is easier, with thousands of unrestricted lakes from which to choose. It still helps to join a club, at least when you start Jet Ski riding, for the help and advice that other members and club staff can give you.

Coastal waters are less restricted, and more of a challenge; but the sea is less predictable and therefore potentially more dangerous. Chapters 3 and 4 have more on this subject, but basically you need competence and commonsense. Always observe local byelaws, as well as the maritime rule of the road.

Wherever you go, ride in company or tell someone reliable of your plans. Also, in your own interests as well as those of other skiers coming after you, avoid annoying other water users. Stick to designated Jet Ski areas and designated boat lanes from the launch site, be considerate and don't act irresponsibly. Irresponsible behaviour has already resulted in personal watercraft being banned from many prime sites.

KITTING YOURSELF OUT

If you hire a Jet Ski, the club or rental operator will probably lend or hire you a wetsuit and a buoyancy aid. But if you are going to buy one, it's worth investing in a more comprehensive set of kit:

A good quality buoyancy aid. A four-buckle vest offers the most protection.

A wetsuit. If you're an all-year rider, you could do with two: a 5mm one-piece steamer or a drysuit for the winter and a two-piece 3mm suit for the summer, with good padding around the knees and shins. As well as keeping you warm they offer some protection: the water can seem like concrete if you come off at speed.

Footwear. You need something that will give you grip on wet rubber and protection from things like sharp stones on the beach. Trainers are fine, or there are specially-made Jet Ski boots which also provide ankle support. Some riders wear wrestling shoes.

Gloves. These prevent blisters and provide better grip, and if you are an all-year skier will be needed to keep your hands warm in winter.

Helmet. Helmets are only mandatory when you're racing, but it's a good idea to wear one even when out for fun. You ought to protect your head, especially at sea, where a fall could end with your colliding with your own Ski. Even on inland waters, there's a case to be made for always wearing a helmet: other personal watercraft may hit you if you fall in their path. And the water is no place to be if you're unconscious after a knock on the head.

But helmets are good for more than head protection, providing warmth in cold weather and making you easier to spot at a distance. Get one that is neither too tight nor too loose, and which is purpose-made for Jet Ski riding: motorcycle helmets are quite unsuitable, being heavy and tending to hold water like a sponge. Jet Ski helmets are comfortable, and have drainage paths and removable liners so they can be washed or dried quicker.

Goggles. These will keep the spray out of your eyes: especially important at sea, where the salt can rub your eyes raw.

Back protector. If you're racing, you need either a back protector or a buoyancy aid with one built in.

RIGHT Always wear the correct clothing – from your toes to your head.

OPPOSITE It's not just racers who should wear goggles – they're recommended for all riders.

TRANSPORT

Jet Ski watercraft might be light, but they still need to be transported around. I've seen them in everything from an estate car to a horse box, but usually owners adopt one of three methods of transporting their craft to and from the water: an open trailer, a box trailer, or some kind of truck, van or pickup.

You'll probably need someone's help to load and unload the Jet Ski from vans and box trailers. A beach trolley will make it easier to transport the Jet Ski from your vehicle to the water's edge. With a trailer, you can back the trailer down the slipway and float the Jet Ski off.

Open trailers

The best trailers are made of galvanised steel tubes welded together, and have a good suspension system and sealed bearings. This is the cheapest method of transporting

your Jet Ski, if you have a family car to tow it behind.

The first thing to do is decide what size trailer you want – single, double or triple. Buy a good one – one that is well balanced and carries a guarantee. The size of the wheel and tyre will depend on how far you plan to tow your Jet Ski: smaller wheels and tyres will have to do a lot more work to keep up with the larger tyres on the tow vehicle. For short jaunts an eight-inch tyre will do fine. Over longer distances heat will build up, commonly resulting in fried bearings or a flat tyre. If you travel more than 100 miles per trip, buy a trailer with at least 12-inch wheels.

Box trailers

Some of the top riders have customised box trailers which carry all the machines and also act as a mobile workshop, changing room and rain shelter. They offer many of

Two of the most popular ways of transporting a Jet Ski – on a trailer ABOVE, and on the back of a pickup LEFT

the advantages of the van or truck, but they are cheaper and you can use them for jobs other than towing a Jet Ski.

If you use a trailer, always carry a spare wheel.

Vans/trucks/pickups

A Jet Ski will fit into an estate car, but it's probably better to use a van or truck. You get more security than with either of the trailer options, but at a price. A pickup, on the other hand, is less secure than a locked box trailer or estate car, so it's important to build in extra counter-theft measures.

Towing

Laws covering the towing of trailers are relatively complex and vary from country to country. Trailer manufacturers or motoring organisations will tell you what is required, but you should also check your car handbook for towing limits. Vehicles towing trailers are usually subject to lower speed limits and other restrictions.

17

Customising your craft may make it less appealing to thieves

SECURITY

Personal watercraft are popular targets for thieves, with hundreds stolen each year. So make your Ski, trailer and vehicle as secure as possible. Lock the boat to the trailer and the trailer to the car whenever you are out on the road.

Accessories that will help protect your Ski from thieves include locking tow bars, wheel clamps, a sturdy padlock and chain, and burglar alarms. An alarm fitted to your garage is ideal, but it may also be worth buying a small vibration-activated one to place inside the boat whenever you leave it unattended.

Another tip is to remove an expensive part like the hood. This will deter a casual thief and make dealers suspicious. Other things you can do to deter thieves or help you get your machine back are:

Mark your craft and engine with your post or Zip code

Make a note of the engine and hull numbers

Get it registered with the sport's governing body

Customise it

Always swing the safety catch across the start button or remove the lanyard when the Jet Ski is not in use. One rider we know

Registering your machine will make it easier to trace if it is stolen

left is boat on a trailer in a pub car park. While he was at lunch, some children casually pressed the green start button. The engine started and ran until it over-heated, and the owner came back to find his engine seized.

You probably won't be able to get insurance if you do silly things like this

INSURANCE

With the increase in the number of personal watercraft thefts it is important to get good insurance. This isn't always straightforward. Insurance companies who charge less may be able to undercut their competitors because they pay out less; you won't find out until you have to make a claim. Shop around for quotes, then ask other Jet Ski riders who they are insured with – and if they've had any problems with claims.

You will need a comprehensive policy that covers all these risks:

Theft: from the garage, while in transit, or by the water

Fire

Accidental damage: in use or while stored

Use abroad

Third party liability. A mishandled personal watercraft can do a lot of damage at 40mph, so you should look for a minimum of £250,000/$500,000 cover.

If you go racing, you'll probably need extra cover on top of all this.

CHAPTER 3 GETTING AFLOAT

BEFORE LAUNCHING

Most of these jobs can and should be done before you leave home if you want to avoid wasting time at the launch site, and possibly a wasted journey.

1. Check the hull for damage, and check the operation of throttle, steering and, if fitted, the ignition cut-out device.

2. Open the hood to ventilate the engine compartment, and use a sponge to soak up any water or fuel in the bottom. Check for fuel or oil leaks, and check battery fluid and oil levels. Then close the hood, making sure all the latches are secure.

3. Loosen the fuel filler cap to relieve any pressure that may have built up in the tank. Top up the fuel: this will avoid your spilling the oily mix over the slipway or into the water later on. Be careful not to over-tighten the fuel filler cap, which may crack the thread and let water into the tank.

4. Check intakes, jet and bilge pump nozzles for obstructions.

5. Make sure you have got all your gear, and that it's in good condition – especially the buoyancy aid and the fire extinguisher.

6. If you use a trailer, check the lights, tyres and bearings, and secure the Jet Ski to the trailer with tie-downs before you take to the road.

7. Get a weather forecast that tells you the sea condition in coastal areas, and don't go out if you're not confident you can handle the conditions.

LAUNCHING

The easiest way to get your craft into the water is to back it down a slipway on a trailer and float it off. Remember to remove the trailer light board before you begin reversing, and don't hog the slipway. Open the hood to ventilate the engine compartment of any car exhaust fumes it may have drawn in on the driver.

Check the ramp first, to make sure it's wide enough, not too steep for the rig and with a reasonably firm surface. If it's slippery or wet, take along a couple of wheel chocks in case the rig starts to slide. It is best to have someone outside the car to direct you as you back down the slipway.

When you reach the water's edge, stop, remove the tie-downs and either attach handling lines to the Jet Ski or get someone standing by ready to float the boat off.

Back the trailer into the water, avoiding complete immersion of the wheels if possible: the wheels will have become very hot on the drive to the slipway, and as the hub cools on immersion, water will be drawn into the bearings with potentially disastrous effects.

Float the Jet Ski off the trailer, and drive back up the slipway. Practise on a quiet day so you know what you are doing when it is busy and there are other water users trying to launch their craft before the tide goes out.

ABOVE If you transport your Jet Ski in a van or pickup, ask a friend to help you get it to the water

LEFT The easiest way to launch your personal watercraft is by backing the trailer down the slip

Using a beach trolley to launch a Jet Ski

If you're on your own you may be able to drag your Jet Ski down to the water like this

If you have a van, you can use a beach trolley to get your machine to the water's edge. Alternatively, two people can carry it, one each end.

Once at the water's edge you can drag the Jet Ski into the water. Lift either the front or the back end out of the water – the back end's lighter – and tow the machine out. Once clear of the shallows, bounce the back of the craft up and down a few times to dislodge any stones or other debris that may have collected near the impeller.

Point the Jet Ski into the waves. Don't start the engine until you are in about 2ft of water, to avoid stones being sucked into the impeller. Then get it well and truly warmed up before you take off.

To recover the craft, you reverse the launch procedure, i.e. you float the craft back on the trailer or carry it back to your van.

STARTING OFF

Before starting off, check that the fuel valve is on, and that the starter interlock switch (by the stop/start control) is set to run. Don't go out with the fuel switched over to RES (reserve): if you run out of fuel, you won't be able to get back to shore again.

On the first start of the day, warm the engine for 15 seconds out of the water. This saves load on the starter and battery. Then, once in the water, allow two to three minutes for full warm-up.

Stand in the water next to the boat, well away from the jet nozzle. Pull the choke knob out all the way, grasp the right handlebar with your right hand and apply a small amount of throttle.

With your left hand push the green start button on the left handlebar. Release it as soon as the engine starts, but don't keep it

TOP RIGHT Riding a Jet Ski is an energetic business, so warm up well before you go out

BELOW RIGHT Always start in knee-deep water

ABOVE Use your left hand to press the start and stop buttons and your right hand to control the thumb or finger throttle. This photo also shows the location of the choke.

pressed for more than five seconds at a time if the engine is reluctant to get going. If it won't start, wait for fifteen seconds before trying again. Don't under any circumstances press the starter while the engine is running or the starter motor spinning: you can damage or jam the starter.

As soon as the engine fires, push in the choke knob. Allow two or three minutes warm-up, blipping the throttle occasionally to prevent fouling of the plugs.

Within fifteen seconds of the engine starting – or immediately if the boat has already been out – there should be a telltale stream of water coming out of the by-pass outlet at the back of the Ski. No telltale means there is no coolant circulating round the engine, in which case you should shut down and investigate the reason before the engine overheats.

If the engine refuses to start, carry out the checks in the Troubleshooting Guide, towards the end of Chapter 4.

Your first start will be a shallow-water one. Once the engine is running, move round to the back of the Ski, grasp the handlebars and put one knee up on to the riding platform. Don't put your whole weight on it yet, or you'll capsize.

Check that the water ahead is clear of swimmers, debris or other traffic. Straighten the handlebars, apply the throttle and accelerate rapidly: the Ski won't be either steerable or stable enough to take your weight until the engine starts to deliver thrust.

As the craft accelerates, pull your body up on to the riding platform and onto your knees, using your elbows on the raised edges for leverage. For the moment, keep your weight low and as far forward as you can without interfering with handlebar movement.

At first the bow will rise, but as the Ski increases speed, the nose will drop and the hull will level out on to the plane. Heavier riders will take longer to get up. Once up, you will find you can ease off the throttle substantially if you want without coming off the plane.

You will also have to master the deep-water start for those times when you and the Jet Ski part company. For obvious reasons it is more difficult than the shallow-water one, especially for heavier or unfit riders, but is no real problem. Lie in the water behind the Ski, with your hands on the handlebars, start the engine, accelerate, and pull yourself up and onto the riding platform as before.

The deepwater start. Lie with your thighs resting on the edge of the tray. When you are going fast enough for the machine to support you, pull yourself up

For your first ride, stay on your knees with the handlepole down while you get used to the feel of the machine. You shouldn't lean on the handlebars, since the pole rests on the hood and may damage it.

The position of your body in the tray drastically alters the handling of the machine. The most common fault among beginners is to position themselves too far back on the machine, with the result that the Jet Ski hops or porpoises along, no matter how fast or slow they travel. The answer is to get your knees further forward and even lean forward slightly until the porpoising stops.

STOPPING

There are two ways to stop the Jet Ski. Pressing the red stop button will kill the engine instantly: the boat will come off the plane and the water will do the rest, bringing it to a halt within a few yards. For a more gradual effect, cut the revs right back and the boat will glide to a halt. The rear will usually submerge on stopping, depending on the weight of the rider, and this can be used to advantage: for an immediate stop, experts shift their weight towards the rear at the same time as they kill the engine.

Don't forget that you lose thrust, and therefore also steering, the moment the engine stops. You also lose steering when the engine is idling, so if you need to keep directional control you will have to ease the throttle back slowly to a full stop. If you are heading back to shore, always stop the engine and dismount in at least two feet of water to prevent stones etc being sucked into the impeller.

If the engine stops of its own accord, it's probably run out of fuel. Switch the valve from ON to RES and press the start button again: don't operate the choke knob.

TURNING

On the turn, the Jet Ski behaves very much like a motorcycle. You have to lean into a turn to keep your balance and to pull the boat round; but in addition, because no thrust means no steering, you need to keep the revs up. The higher the throttle setting, the faster you will turn; if the engine is cut back to idle, the boat won't turn at all.

As you approach a corner you should shift your weight towards the side of the Ski that will be on the inside of the turn. Some top riders hang their bodies over the edge of the platform for maximum effect and bite, but this is not a good idea for novices as you are more likely to fall if the Ski slides wide.

Always, always look before you turn. There may be other water users nearby.

The basic body positions for left and right turns

Find a comfortable foot position and experiment by changing it as you perform different manoeuvres.

STANDING

Once you have gained confidence, try standing up. Maintaining a steady speed, raise the handlepole slightly and place one foot near the front of the riding platform. Balance yourself and slowly rise to a standing position, bringing the handlebar up with you as you rise.

Standing, you will need to experiment with the positioning of your feet to get the best out of your Jet Ski. Don't move too far back, or the nose will rise and you will start to porpoise. Conversely, bringing your weight too far forward may cause the back of the Jet Ski to break away, putting you

into an uncontrolled tail slide.

There are actually three postures you will need to practise: one for the straights, two for the corners. On the straight you will need to use your body weight to trim the Ski, positioning your centre of gravity over the centre of the craft and crouching to reduce wind resistance. If the crouch position makes your back ache, you could try fitting a handlepole spring which reduces the weight of the pole.

Find a position that is comfortable and gives you confidence on the turn. Some people are happy with their feet together; others, like me, prefer one foot in front of the other. Some riders move their feet around depending on which way they are turning. I put my right foot forward for a right-hand turn and left foot in front when I'm turning to the left.

The smaller and lighter the rider the easier it should be to perform basic manoeuvres. But heavier riders should not be put off – it might just help if they use a 550 instead of a 300 or 440. Once under way and on the plane, heavier riders should have no problems.

Don't worry about falling off your Jet Ski – everybody does it. As they say, 'If you're not falling, you're not learning'

FALLING OFF

Everyone falls off a Jet Ski from time to time: it's part of the fun of the sport. But, as in judo, you should know how to fall.

Firstly, don't try to hang on to the handlebars. This will stop you falling clear, and you may strike the Ski on the way down and injure yourself. Fall outwards, ideally bottom first and legs together, and with your arms over your head.

The moment you let go of the handlebars, the throttle will spring back to idle and the Jet Ski will start to circle slowly back to your position. If you were travelling quite fast immediately before the fall, there may be a delay before the boat slows sufficiently to start circling, but you shouldn't have a long swim to catch up with it. Swim towards the circle and wait for the Ski to come around.

If the Ski capsizes completely, the engine

will stall. Swim up behind it, grasp the side fins or the hull bottom and turn it upright. It is essential that when righting a Jet Ski you turn it clockwise: i.e. from upside down, to lying on its left side, to fully upright. If you do it the other way water can run into the exhaust and into the engine cylinders.

Whatever you do to the Ski, it won't sink, because the hull is filled with closed-cell foam that keeps it buoyant even if the engine compartment fills with water. However, in the latter case the bow will remain submerged until you can empty the engine compartment, which you should do ashore, again by tipping the machine on its left side.

If the engine fails to start after a capsize, it may have taken in water through the carburettor or fuel tank. Tow the Ski ashore and drain the engine immediately (see Chapter 4) to prevent damage to the crankshaft bearings and other internal parts.

Falling off frequently can be very tiring. Don't overdo your first few sessions: take regular breaks to allow your muscles to recover, and stop the moment you find climbing back aboard difficult.

SKIING OFFSHORE

Skiing on coastal waters demands more skill and stamina to cope with waves. Make sure you listen to the weather forecast, and know what the tide and local currents are doing. And if the wind starts to get up, head back ashore immediately.

Sea water is denser than fresh water, with the result that the Ski will float higher and handle differently. In rough water you will probably find it best to change your normal straight-line riding stance so that you have both feet towards the back of the Ski. This will keep the nose up and the pump well immersed.

In offshore conditions the engine compartment may take in more water than the standard bilge pump can cope with. If you intend to do a lot of sea skiing, it will be worth investing in an electric bilge pump. Another worthwhile investment is a small pack of flares which can be kept in the fire extinguisher compartment and used to signal for help in the event of a problem.

SAFETY

A Jet Ski is inherently safe, but in irresponsible hands it can do a great deal of damage to other water users. Always think safe and act responsibly: don't travel at high speed within 60 yards of any other water user, always keep an eye out for debris, buoys etc and obey any local regulations.

Check with the harbourmaster if you're not sure what restrictions there are on the

ABOVE RIGHT When riding offshore it often helps to stand well back to keep the back of the craft down and the pump in the water

BELOW RIGHT Jet Skis are highly manoeuvrable, so almost everything else has right of way over them. But always observe the speed limits or you might attract the attention of cops like Tubbs and Crocket from Miami Vice

use of Skis in his area. Speeding, inconsiderate behaviour and failure to use designated Ski areas will get you banned or fined, and may result in a general ban on personal watercraft in that area.

The international rules that apply to ski boats, large cruisers or other power boats also apply to you. Since it's likely that you'll be sharing the waterways with other craft, you should know what to do.

As a general principle, less manoeuvrable craft have right of way over the rest. So power gives way to sail, small gives way to large – which means that personal watercraft should keep clear of everything. If you are overtaking another craft, keep well clear and pass them on the right; and if you're approaching another head-on, the rule is that each of you alters course to the right.

When two craft are converging at right angles, the left one must slow down or change course to pass behind the vessel approaching from the right

When two boats are converging on each other at right angles, the left one must slow down or change course to pass behind the vessel approaching from the right. The boat on the right is expected to maintain a steady course and speed.

In narrow channels, stay to the right whenever possible.

Despite the water all around, fire afloat can be lethal. You should know how to get at your extinguisher, and how to operate it. If you have a fire, stop the engine and try to put it out, but don't take any risks: it's better to swim clear and wait for rescue.

Never ski alone. At least one other Ski should be present to act as a rescue craft in the event of an accident or breakdown.

Finally, don't ride your Jet Ski under the influence of drink or drugs, or between dusk and dawn.

At the end of the day rev the engine to get rid of water from the exhaust, and wash the machine down

AT THE END OF THE DAY

When you've finished with the Ski for the day, you should drain the exhaust system of water. Bring the Ski ashore, and lift it 10-12in by the rear. Then start the engine and rev it gently until no more water comes out of the exhaust. Don't keep it running for more than 15 seconds, or the engine may overheat. Never run the engine at maximum revs out of the water.

If there is a lot of water in the engine compartment, tip it over on its left side (with a towel underneath to prevent damage to the glassfibre) to drain. Then wipe the engine compartment out with a sponge or cloth and replace the hood.

Using the boat in seawater will leave salt deposits in the cooling system which should be flushed out with fresh water before they have a chance to build up and clog the tubes. At the same time, the engine compartment itself should be hosed down with clean tap water to prevent the salt from corroding external engine parts and. fittings.

CHAPTER 4

MAINTENANCE AND IMPROVEMENT

DOING IT YOURSELF

Knowing your machine inside and out will help you get the most out of it, and the best way to learn is to do your own maintenance. It will also ensure you don't lose time on the water.

All bodywork should be cleaned, especially after sea use, with soapy water. Every now and again use a good silicone wax to seal it and protect the glassfibre.

HULL

Check the hull regularly for knocks, dents or exposed glassfibre. Deep scratches or chips should be filled with gelcoat filler and rubbed down. This is to keep the water out of the laminate: if water gets in, the glassfibre can literally come apart at the seams.

Shallow scratches along the length of the hull are not really that important. Actually, a rougher surface will make the Ski handle better: if it's too smooth underneath, the Ski will slide around too much. Champion Larry Rippenkroeger remembers when he worked for Performance Jet Ski owner Ed Miller: "He was a real stickler. The Skis were never to be ridden before the race. No test riding. The bottoms were as clean and shiny as the tops, and had no scoop grates, which give a lot of straight-line stability. Those boats were unbelievably fast, but they handled terribly." So one day he ran his Ski up the beach and scuffed the bottom. It handled much better after that!

RIGHT The 1991 Kawasaki 550SX, and an exploded view of the same machine. The diagram at the bottom shows how the exhaust system works

BELOW Major overhauls and repairs are best left to the professionals.

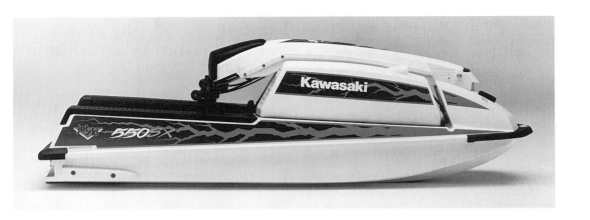

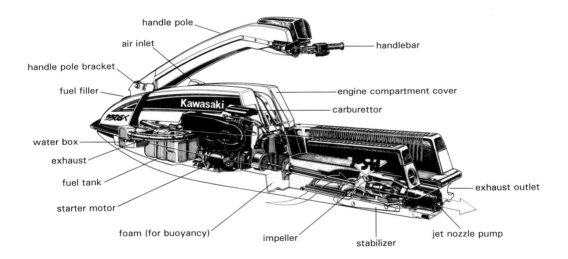

handle pole

air inlet

handlebar

handle pole bracket

fuel filler

engine compartment cover

carburettor

water box

exhaust

fuel tank

starter motor

exhaust outlet

foam (for buoyancy)

impeller

stabilizer

jet nozzle pump

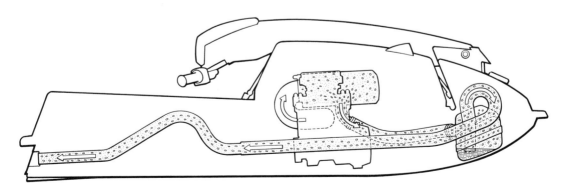

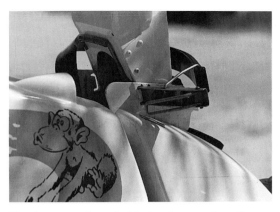

Use the stop on the end of the hood strap to keep the hood up when you are working on the engine, and when you store your Jet Ski

Make sure all the nuts and bolts are tight on hull fittings such as the scoop grate and ride plate. They have a tendency to vibrate undone.

BOND LINE

This is where the hull is joined to the nose cone and the riding platform. Although one of the strongest parts of the Ski, it can be damaged by a side impact. Early models had the standard bumper simply glued on, with the result that it fell off easily, but on later models the bumper is further secured by screws.

NOSE CONE

If you use your Jet Ski extensively in the sea (for wave jumping etc), the nose cone – which absorbs most of the forces that the Ski sustains – will start to crack. When buying a secondhand Ski, it is always worth checking the nose cone for cracks across the bottom and around the pole bracket. Look out in particular for cracks that go all the way through and weaken the structure.

It's difficult to repair the nose cone because of limited access to the underneath. Replacement is simpler and provides a more lasting solution. Fitting a new nose cone is not difficult. Take the pole off, strip out the cables, saw the top half of the nose cone off, then split it around the bond line using a chisel. Remove it, and clean up the bond line.

Liberally apply a special jointing compound such as Silkflex to the new nose cone to glue it in place. Fit the cone and keep it in place with as many G-clamps as possible. Leave it for at least 48 hours to set, then bolt everything back on again.

If you replace the nose cone, it's always best to use a stainless steel nose bracket to go with it – this will ensure the cone is bolted to the bond line as well as being glued. This added safety measure will reinforce the nose, and also prevent the new nose cone falling off.

HOOD

This is easy to repair if it gets damaged. It is large, easily removable and has no internal components, apart from a water separator just inside the air intake.

You will always get a little water in with the air – more if you are wave-hopping at sea or carrying out freestyle manoeuvres such as submarining. The separator is designed to extract the water from the air before it gets into the engine. Obviously it can't cope with large amounts of water, when the engine bay may flood. This should self-drain, but if you plan on doing a lot of wave-hopping or submarining, fit an electric bilge pump.

Water can also get into the Ski around poorly-fitting hood seals. If they are damaged, replace them. It's an easy and cheap task.

When you store the Ski, always store it

with the hood "cracked". Undo the latches and put a piece of wood under the back to take some pressure off the seals.

HANDLEPOLE

If the handlepole is damaged – other than minor cracks you can get to from the outside – replace it. Because of the loading it takes in use, repairs seldom work. I've seen people hurt themselves badly when poles have snapped.

As the bushes wear, you are likely to get excessive slop in the pole. People tend to tighten the bracket or the pivot bolt to try to reduce some of the side movement. But this is not the answer: it bends the bracket, which will eventually crack. If there is any side movement the best thing to do is to fit a bush set, which is available as an extra. Bore the pole out at the bottom of the pivot, insert the new collars and replace the pole. This will get rid of all the play – you will now have nylon running on the pin instead of just glassfibre.

A pole spring will reduce the weight of the handlepole by up to 60 per cent, making the Jet Ski less tiring and reducing the strain on your back. If you fit a pole spring it's best to fit a backing plate as well. If you don't you are likely to see cracks appearing in the glassfibre.

If you leave the handlepole down all the time, the spring will lose its temper and become less effective. So always store the Ski with its pole up.

The steering pivot base bracket can crack under severe conditions such as wave jumping. Check along its faces. Make sure the steering pivots themselves are greased properly – and that they are not overtight. You should be able to get full movement all the way round.

CABLES

Check that the steering cable is properly secured, and that the throttle cable functions properly, with full movement at either end.

Make sure the cables are not frayed. The throttle cable tends to fray at the nipple; replacement is somewhat fiddly, but it only takes about an hour. Make sure you have the correct amount of slack on the cable, so that when the handlepole moves up or down or the steering moves from lock to lock it won't operate the throttle on its own.

The choke cable is a little easier to refit – the job takes about half an hour. Replacing the steering cable is a much longer job, but they rarely fail.

Cracks at the base of the handlepole weaken the whole unit. Repairs seldom last long, so if your handlepole looks like this, replace it

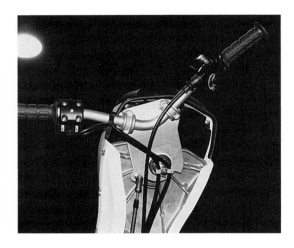

Check the steering cable is properly secured

IMPELLER

The impeller is the equivalent of a propeller on a boat. It can be easily damaged by the smallest stones, so check it regularly for damage, especially if you notice the revs are up for the performance you are getting.

Check the leading edge of the blades – you can do this without removing the scoop grate – to make sure they have a reasonably good cutting edge and also, on a 550, that they shim correctly into the pump itself. If there's too much clearance you will get excessive slip.

Impellers can be cleaned up with a file, providing they are not bent or too severely damaged. They can be repaired in place, but it is best to remove them in order to check that whatever damaged the leading edge hasn't gone through and caused havoc at the back.

Whenever you put your hands anywhere near the impeller, disconnect the battery first.

RIGHT A polished stainless steel impeller

PUMP

The pump acts as a housing for the impeller. On a 550 there is a separate shaft in the housing to which the impeller screws, supported by two bearings and a set of seals. Providing these are greased regularly and the core plug in the centre of the shaft has not fallen out, they should last for a couple of years.

If you do get water into the pump housing or the bearings, the bearing seals will have to be replaced. This is a fairly straightforward job. Remove the pump, take off the end casing, dry out the shaft, then dry the bearings. Replace the seals with a new set. When you replace them, make sure the core plug in the centre of the shaft is securely in place before you put the shaft back. Replace the shaft and end cap, put the impeller back on again and make sure it is shimmed correctly into the cone. When it is all assembled, fill it up with grease.

440s and 300s have a plain bearing in the pump and an impeller screwed to the shaft. These should be greased every time you use the Ski to keep a film of grease between the bearing and shaft. If they're

not greased, the bearing will wear away itself and gradually erode the end of the shaft: then you will have to replace the shaft and the bearing, a long and expensive job.

650 pumps are similar in operation to those on the 550, with a separate shaft spinning in two ball race bearings. The bearings are sealed and don't need greasing, but can be replaced in exactly the same way. Make sure the rubber O-rings on the shaft behind the impeller are in good condition, because they stop water getting into the bearing housing.

When replacing the pump, make sure it is sealed into the body work correctly. Don't overdo the silicone, just enough to seal it. Many people tend to put sealant all the way round, sealing across the pump and across the back of the scoop grate, with the result that when the boat goes into the water it just sits there and revs.

STEERING NOZZLE

The plastic steering nozzle at the rear of the Ski should have full and free movement. It can wear on the pivot pins and jam up on heavy throttle use, so make sure there is not too much play. If there is, replace the pivot pins and steering nozzle. For the small cost, they're not worth repairing.

The back pods next to the steering nozzle act as stabilizers and can be replaced if you damage them. Cut the old ones off and replace them with new ones using a glass-fibre bond. This is a cheap and simple job. The corners do get damaged easily: rub them down and use gelcoat filler to keep the water out. If they are too badly damaged, replace them.

RIGHT Spraying all metal and moving parts with water displacement oil will help keep rust at bay

FIRE EXTINGUISHER/TOOL COMPARTMENT

Keep the seal greased to prevent water getting in and to make it easier to remove the cap.

MATS

The mat on the riding platform takes a battering, so sooner or later you will have to replace it. This is another relatively simple and cheap job. Different mats offer different degrees of durability, grip and brightness.

ENGINE BAY

When you want to get at the engine, keep the handlepole up and out of the way by using the end of the hood strap as a pole stop.

After sea use, always flush out the engine to get rid of salt crystals etc. Wash the engine bay with soapy water, dry out everything and spray with WD40. All the linkages should be greased using a motorcycle chain spray. Check all the hose clips, especially around the exhaust, fuel tank, fuel

pipes. Check all hoses for splits. Clean and check the fuel filter every 20 or 30 hours, cleaning out any water that may have collected in the bottom of the sediment bowl. If there's a lot, find out why: there may be a leak or water in the fuel tank.

Once you have washed the engine bay with soapy water, turn the Ski on its side, hose it down, and mop out the water with a sponge. Run the engine, get it nice and warm (15 secs max) and leave it to dry out. Then spray it with WD40.

If you are constantly spraying things with WD40 you will get an oily build-up inside the hull. Washing it out with soapy water after a session will help break this down. Some people squirt Fairy Liquid round the bottom of the engine bay. When they go out for a ride, any water that's taken in will break down the washing-up liquid and wash it around the bottom, breaking up oil and anything else that's spilt down there. This then exits via the bilge. It keeps the inside nice and clean – and smelling fresh.

Bilge draining system

The engine bay is self-draining, with a drain pipe to the back of the Ski fronted by a non-return valve bolted to the bulkhead. Make sure there is no dirt blocking the valve, using an air line to clear it if necessary. If you have a bored-out steering nozzle, you may need to fit an electric pump.

ENGINE

Although the engine of the Jet Ski is very reliable, it needs attention from time to time to keep it at peak performance.

Servicing

To carry out full services you will need a grease gun, torque wrench, various service tools, your Owner's Handbook and a certain amount of mechanical knowhow. If you haven't got these, leave the job to your local dealer – who, incidentally, can also supply a very detailed workshop manual to suit each Kawasaki Jet Ski model.

First service – after three tankfuls. The head should be tightened down to the correct torque setting, and all nuts and bolts checked. Make sure everything that is supposed to move does, and that everything that is supposed to be firmly fixed is. Give the dealer a list of any complaints you may have.

Every 15–20 hours – Check that nothing is worn out or about to break. Grease all points. Check the torque on the cylinder head nuts, making sure the head is tightened down to the standard setting in the correct sequence.

Filter elements tend to deteriorate, and should be checked every service. Wash them out with a high-flashpoint solvent and blow them clear. After a year's service, replace them because they have a tendency to break up, with the risk that the engine will suck the pieces in.

Check the cylinder pressure with a pressure gauge. Take both spark plugs out, insert them into their caps and ground them on a metal part of the engine. Screw in the gauge, hold the throttle fully open and press the starter button for about five or six seconds. Read off the pressure. Then do the same on the other cylinder.

There should be no more than about 10 per cent discrepancy between the two readings. Ask your local dealer what the pressure should be on your engine. Obviously, if the heads have been skimmed or there are any other modifications, the cylinder pressure will be higher. If you bought the Ski secondhand and the previous owner had the head skimmed, it's worth finding out how much he's had it skimmed and what the original cylinder pressures were.

If the cylinder pressure is low the piston

The engine of a Kawasaki 550SX

rings should be replaced. On 440s, pre-1987 550s and 650s this can be done with the engine in place. On post-1987 550s, it's more of a struggle and you have to take off the exhaust system. You're probably wiser to remove the engine – it will save time in the long run and make it easier to work on. Remove the cylinder head and cylinder barrel with the exhaust system and carburettor still in place. Replace the rings and bolt it all back together again. Put the engine back and re-align it.

Carburettor

The purpose of the carburettor is to feed the engine with the correct metered fuel/air ratio for all throttle settings. You shouldn't need to keep adjusting it.

Many of the problems arise through incorrect mix ratios. You will see people with a 20-litre fuel can tip their oil bottle up at a 45-degree angle for nine seconds and say that's their measured amount of oil. The only way to measure oil properly is in a jug, so you can be sure you have the same ratio every time. Too much oil will make it run too lean, too little oil will make it run too rich.

People who have not mixed the fuel correctly often make the mistake of playing around with the carburettor screws to make it run right.

Stick to the same ratio, and the same carburettor setting. Once the carburettor is set for that ratio you should never need to set it again, except in extreme atmospheric or temperature conditions.

Carburettor maintenance is very straightforward. The only thing you get from time to time is a blocked primary jet, particularly on X-2s, where the jet sits right at the bottom and towards the back of the fuel chamber. Anything that goes into the carburettor will go straight into the primary, which being a hole of probably no more than 0.5mm in diameter can easily get blocked with foreign matter. 650SXs, although fitted with the same carburettor, don't seem to be afflicted with the same problem.

So, if you have difficulty in starting the engine of an X-2, or if it will only run on choke, suspect a blocked primary. In that case, take off the carburettor, strip it down, blow the jets out and put it back together again.

440 and 550 carbs are slightly different – they don't have removable jets. Slow running on a 550 can often be cured by running it rich for a short while: undo the screw about four turns. This often draws out any foreign matter in the drillings. Make sure you return the screw to its normal setting afterwards.

The fuel chamber diaphragm loses its strength very quickly and should be changed every 20–30 hours to keep the flow up. If it becomes weak you will lose fuel out of the chamber, and performance will suffer.

Check the butterfly screws, especially the ones on the choke, which tend to come loose. If they do loosen up, remove the choke completely and fit a primer kit. Once the screws start to come loose, the heads can break off and get sucked into the engine, where they can cause a great deal of damage.

Make sure the throttle linkages and throttle shaft move freely but are not too sloppy. If they are, the only thing you can do is replace the carburettor, unless you know an engineer who can make up some

bushes. But it is usually just as easy to replace the whole carburettor. That's probably the only time you will need to do this.

To service the carburettor, blow it through with an airline – the nozzle should be at right angles to the jets to avoid damaging them – then replace diaphragms and gaskets.

Air filter/flame arrester

The standard air filter is an efficient flame arrester and easily copes with any flashback through the carburettor. It also helps prevent water getting into the carburettor. But it restricts the amount of air flowing

An old, dirty air filter and flame arrester will need replacing; otherwise the air flow through the unit will be restricted

down through the venturi (the tunnel through the centre of the carburettor), and as it gets older and more clogged the air flow will be reduced even further. Check it every service, and if it seems clogged replace it.

Fuel system
Every once in a while check the fuel lines right through to the tap itself. This is especially important with early machines, where the filter was installed downline of the fuel tap, so any foreign matter in the tank would get sucked up into the fuel pipes and block the fuel valve.

Every now and again blow the pipes out with an air line. On later machines the fuel filter is in the tank on the pick-up so this problem doesn't arise.

Electrics
The electrics on a Jet Ski are usually fairly reliable. The only thing you really have to keep a check on is the battery, which should be fully charged before every session. Put it on a trickle charge, no more than about 1 amp/hr. If you've got a dual-purpose charger, 6 volts will do. Keep a check on the battery terminals and keep them greased. Where the battery and start cables are fixed to the solenoid, make sure the terminals are greased and nipped up.

Standard batteries are diaphragm-venting so the battery acid won't escape or water leak into the cells when the Ski is turned upside down. Sea water can kill a battery in minutes if it gets inside, so don't try to save money on cheaper alternatives.

Several different types of spark plug are available. The standard spark plug for a 550 is NGK's BR8ES (B8ES in USA), but many riders use BR7ES, which is a slightly hotter plug and may make starting easier.

Replace plugs every ten hours for your own peace of mind. It's not so bad if you ride on a lake and are never too far from the shore, but if you get stuck in the sea, two miles offshore, you'll have a long swim back.

Some of the early spark plug caps tended to break up inside, so it's worth the extra cost of fitting the later-type rubber caps. Spray everything with WD40 and make sure all the couplings are tight.

Water/cooling pipes
These need to be flushed out regularly, especially if you use the Ski at sea. When you flush the system out it is best to back-flush it so the water runs backwards through the engine, which gets rid of any sediment build-up in the water line. If you have an early Ski that uses plastic clips, replace them with stainless steel jubilee clips. The plastic ones tend to break.

Replace water hoses every 1–2 years or whenever you see cracks appearing. They will need replacing more frequently if you take your Ski to sea.

Exhaust system
The standard Jet Ski exhaust system is 100 per cent reliable. The only maintenance it needs is occasional replacement of the gaskets – and that's just as a safety precaution. Top technician Alan Hesselden says: "It's best to replace them once a year with the rest of the gaskets on the engine. Gaskets do wear out and they are inexpensive to replace."

Crankshaft, crankcase and seals
These are very reliable provided you carry out the correct engine maintenance procedures after use. Most crankshaft failures are due to rust. Any rust on the big end will cause it to fail within hours, so it is very important to make sure there is no water in the engine. Replace the crankshaft seal every 50/60 hours.

Most of the other bottom-end work is labour-intensive, requires special tools and is probably best left to your dealer. Crankshaft, big end and main bearing replacement is possible on 440s because the big end pin can be pushed out of both flywheels. On a 550, if the big end fails, throw the crankshaft away because the pin is part of one of the flywheels. If the big ends are good, all main bearings can be replaced without any problem at all.

Drive coupling

The drive coupling rubber under the splashguard should last a couple of years provided that the engine is lined correctly to the shaft. Make sure everything is in line: again, this is especially important with earlier models. You can tell if it's not in line, when a little line of black rubber will appear under the drive coupling. If you leave it too long the coupling will wear away or break and you will get a bad clacking sound. So it's worth taking the casing off every now and again to check this. If the rubber shows any signs of wear, replace it.

Drive line

The driveshaft is supported between the crank and the impeller by two bearings and four seals in a cast aluminium housing. As long as these are greased regularly using the grease point provided, you should not have any problems for at least two years.

Replacing the driveshaft bearings is a long job. On the 440 you have to take the pump off, unscrew the impeller, then take the engine out, undo the front casing, and pull the whole lot out through the engine bay. On the 550 you can leave the pump housing in place, because it's splined into a separate shaft, but you still have to remove the engine to replace the bearings.

When you replace all the driveshaft bearings, if you don't remove the housing you won't have any realignment problems, provided everything was in line in the first place. If you do remove the housing, which

Always use the right tools for the job

is shimmed into the bulkhead, you will have to check the position of the shaft relative to the engine and to the housing, shim up accordingly, reseal with silicone sealant, and bolt it back on again.

When you have the whole assembly back together again, fill it up with grease until you hear the grease squeeze out underneath the seals. This should also be done about every 10–20 hours' use.

Engine mountings

You can soon tell if the engine mountings are broken because everything starts vibrating. If your Ski is over two years old, check the mountings regularly and replace them if you see any signs of degrading.

Fuel/oil

The best fuel for a Jet Ski is super unleaded, which runs a lot cooler than other fuels.

Many types of oil are available. For standard Jet Ski watercraft most brands of marine two-stroke are fine, but biodegradable ones are kinder on the environment. Use the manufacturers' recommended mix ratios – usually 40/50:1. For racing, synthetic or semi-synthetic oils are best, and should be mixed at 50:1 ratios.

If you use a non-marine mineral or synthetic-based oil, make sure that you always use up all the fuel in your tank: any mix left in the tank will absorb water, making the engine hard to start and reducing performance. Marine oil has additives in it to stop it from absorbing water, so you can use it even if it's been stored for a while – the water will lie in the bottom of the tank rather than dissolve into the mix itself.

WINTERISING

Fine-weather Jet Ski users should spend a few hours 'winterising' their machine before putting it away at the end of the season. Don't just abandon your craft in the back of the garage in September and forget about it until the sun starts to shine again in May or June. You'll find the battery is dead, or bits are corroded or broken and need replacing before you can use it again. Meanwhile, the salt water that has lain there all winter has done untold damage.

A couple of hours spent getting the Ski ready for its winter lay-up will pay dividends in the spring.

The first thing to do is wash the machine in a mild detergent solution – outside and in the engine bay as well. Then dry the compartment thoroughly.

Flush the bilge, cooling and exhaust systems, and clean the bilge strainer ·if fitted. Check that the pinhole in the bilge

Make sure you fill up with the correct fuel-oil mix

breather is not blocked. Using an air line, blow any water out of the cooling and bilge hoses. Examine all cooling, bilge and exhaust hoses for cracks, perishing or rubbing and all hose clamps. Replace any suspect hoses straight away.

Pour or pump the remaining fuel from the fuel tank. Remember to leave either the fuel pick-up fitting or the fuel cap loose to prevent condensation forming in the tank. Drain and clean out all filters, sediment bowls and water traps in the fuel lines. Start the engine and run it to clear the remaining fuel from the fuel lines. Remember, running an engine out of water for more than 15 seconds can cause serious damage.

Remove the flame arrester element,

lubricate where necessary and replace. Remove the spark plugs and put the plug caps back on, then lay the plugs on the engine to earth them. Pour one ounce, about a teaspoonful, of engine oil into each plug hole, then turn the engine over briefly with the starter to distribute the oil on the cylinder walls. Replace the spark plugs and caps. Remove the exhaust hose from the waterbox and replace. Pour a small amount of antifreeze into the waterbox because you can never get rid of all the water.

Remove the battery from the machine and wash the outside with a mild solution of baking soda in water to neutralise any spilt acid. Top up the battery with distilled water, grease both terminals thoroughly and store in a cool dry place. Charge the battery about once a month at the recommended rate.

Wax polish the outside of the hull and apply a silicone spray to all metal parts outside and inside the machine to prevent damp from attacking them during storage.

Lubricate all cables, linkages and grease all bearings as specified in your handbook. Replace the engine cover loosely, allowing air to circulate freely around the engine bay to prevent condensation.

If you have a trailer, it will also merit some attention. Check the bearings to see if they need replacing or adjusting. Check each wheel in turn by lifting the wheel clear off the ground and checking for play by grasping the wheel top and bottom and rocking. If there is excess play, adjust the bearing.

While the wheel is clear off the ground, spin the wheel. If the bearing 'rumbles' the bearing is certainly due for replacement. Wash the trailer chassis down and check all fittings for tightness. Grease all moving parts, including the hitch. If brakes are fitted, check that they work and are correctly adjusted. Check tyre pressures, and check tyres for cuts, cracks and bulges. Re-

place if in doubt. Mudguards that are cracked, loose or missing should also be replaced. Check that the light board works properly.

A little time and effort in autumn will save a lot of time and money at the start of the next season. If you haven't the time to carry out a proper winterisation programme yourself, let your local dealer do it for you.

TROUBLESHOOTING

Most mechanical problems you are likely to come up against with a Jet Ski can be dealt with simply and swiftly using the tool kit supplied with the craft. Use the troubleshooting guide opposite to identify the problem.

Draining the engine
Water in the engine compartment is no real problem. Water in the engine itself is, and it is essential to drain it immediately – or at the very least within a couple of hours of immersion. Pull the Ski ashore, remove the engine cover and take out the spark plugs, grounding their leads against the metal of the engine.

Now turn the Ski upside down (as usual, turning it on to its left side first), with a towel or two underneath to prevent damage to the gelcoat. Allow the water to drain out of cylinders through the spark plug holes.

That removes some of the water, but by no means all. Keeping your hands well clear of the jet pump intake, open the throttle and give the engine a few turns with the start button. More water will come out of the cylinders.

Turn the Ski back upright, open the throttle and crank the engine again. This will eject any water cupped in the pistons.

Keep cranking, first upside down, then the right way up, until no more water comes out. Turn the Ski upright again, spray a

TROUBLESHOOTING GUIDE

If this procedure does not isolate your problem, see your JET SKI dealer or refer to the Service Manual.

TROUBLE

CAUSE

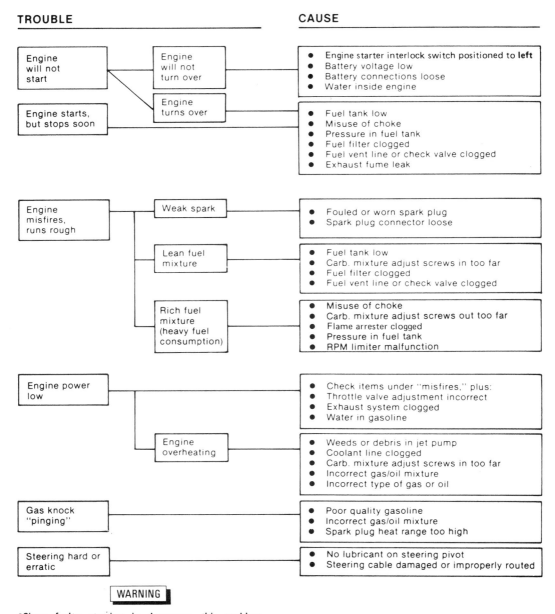

Engine will not start

Engine will not turn over
- Engine starter interlock switch positioned to **left**
- Battery voltage low
- Battery connections loose
- Water inside engine

Engine starts, but stops soon

Engine turns over
- Fuel tank low
- Misuse of choke
- Pressure in fuel tank
- Fuel filter clogged
- Fuel vent line or check valve clogged
- Exhaust fume leak

Engine misfires, runs rough

Weak spark
- Fouled or worn spark plug
- Spark plug connector loose

Lean fuel mixture
- Fuel tank low
- Carb. mixture adjust screws in too far
- Fuel filter clogged
- Fuel vent line or check valve clogged

Rich fuel mixture (heavy fuel consumption)
- Misuse of choke
- Carb. mixture adjust screws out too far
- Flame arrester clogged
- Pressure in fuel tank
- RPM limiter malfunction

Engine power low
- Check items under "misfires," plus:
- Throttle valve adjustment incorrect
- Exhaust system clogged
- Water in gasoline

Engine overheating
- Weeds or debris in jet pump
- Coolant line clogged
- Carb. mixture adjust screws in too far
- Incorrect gas/oil mixture
- Incorrect type of gas or oil

Gas knock "pinging"
- Poor quality gasoline
- Incorrect gas/oil mixture
- Spark plug heat range too high

Steering hard or erratic
- No lubricant on steering pivot
- Steering cable damaged or improperly routed

WARNING

○**Since faulty steering is dangerous, this problem should be examined by an authorized JET SKI dealer.**

rust inhibitor such as WD40 or Belray 6-in-1 into the cylinders, clean and spray the spark plugs and refit them. Then try starting the engine.

If the engine will not start, have another go at cleaning the spark plugs. If it still won't go, suspect water in the fuel system. Remove and clean the fuel sediment bowl and filter, drain the tank by pump or syphon and refill with fresh fuel.

Finally, remove the plug from the magneto cover, and spray inhibitor into the cover to dry out the electrics and prevent rust. Replace the engine cover and secure it, launch the Ski and run the engine for several minutes to dry out any remaining water and blow foreign matter (like salt) out through the exhaust.

TUNING YOUR JET SKI

Everyone wants to go faster. Whether you are a racer or simply go Jet Ski riding for fun, once you get the hang of the machine you will want add that touch of extra speed to keep you at the front of the pack. But think first.

All stock personal watercraft can be made to go faster and handle better. But there are good reasons for standard models being built the way they are, and it's important to remember that any modifications you make to the engine are likely to affect its reliability, and will negate any warranty that is in force. They might also affect your ability to handle the machine: don't try boosting the power if you aren't confident you can cope with the sometimes arm-wrenching results.

Comfort and handling
Bolt-on goodies aren't likely to compromise the reliability of your machine, so they usually constitute the first improvements owners make to their craft. There are many available, from high-grip replacement tray mats and customising kits to electric bilge pumps, many of which we covered earlier in this chapter.

In addition, you may want to consider fitting straighter handlebars. These will give you freer movement while still allowing you to apply full lock, and increase your control of the Ski, especially when wave-jumping or tight cornering. And while on the subject of handlebars, many riders also swap the thumb throttle for a finger throttle and add better quality handlebar grips.

Two bolt-ons for the hull that will improve performance are a racing scoop grate and a racing ride plate. The grate has two bars instead of the normal three, increasing water flow to the impeller, while the ride plate will improve stability at speed.

A trick steer is a simple bracket that fits on to the steering plate, effectively altering the gearing between handlebars and jet nozzle so that the same movement of the bars gives a nozzle movement of up to 50% more than with the standard set-up.

Tuning
To improve performance, the first step is usually to increase compression. This can be done by skimming the head or buying a high-compression racing head, but you can achieve a small increase at much less cost by simply replacing the head gasket with a thinner one. If you do opt for a skimmed head, it may be worth modifying or replacing the pistons and porting the cylinders as well.

Improving fuel flow will also give you better performance. Change the air filter/flame arrester for one that lets more air through, and either buy a bigger carburettor or upgrade the standard one by changing the needle float valve and boring out the main jet.

The exhaust system needs to be looked at. You can't modify the standard fitting,

Regular maintenance is rewarded by good performance

that enters the engine cooling system leaves through the exhaust. It collects at the front of the Ski in the water box, acting as a baffle and cooling the exhaust before it exits. The standard water box keeps noise down, and so is best for all but top racing machines: otherwise, the gain in performance is not worth the extra noise annoyance and loss of usage areas − or the extra maintenance.

Finally, turn your attention to the drive system. It is no good fitting an extremely powerful engine and expecting it to drive the standard jet unit: when you pour on the increased power all you will get is a lot of air round the blades, and if you're lucky a tiny increase in top speed. There are numerous varieties of high-performance impeller available that can be fitted to the standard pump unit to increase thrust and water flow.

If you opt for a higher-pitch impeller, top speed will increase, but at the expense of acceleration. The solution is to bore out the jet nozzle, which has the same effect as lowering the pitch again. You get roughly half a degree of pitch by trimming 1mm off the nozzle diameter. As an example, a Ski with a 16-degree impeller and a nozzle bored out by 1mm will enjoy the same acceleration as a Ski with a 15.5-degree impeller and stock nozzle, but will retain the top speed provided by the steeper pitch.

There are two types of improvement you can make to the pump − blueprinting or extrude-honing. Blueprinting is perfecting a factory produced item to a standard as high as the original blueprint. With a pump this usually means removing excess weld from seams and joints, checking the impeller alignment and ensuring all the tolerances are correct. Extrude-honing means polishing all the internal surfaces of the pump. This is done by forcing abrasive pastes through the pump under pressure, resulting in a practically glass-smooth internal chamber to allow an unhindered flow of water.

but you can buy racing exhausts which, while expensive, will provide you with a greater increase in power than any other modification can. Remember, though, that racing exhausts make more noise − and more noise results in less water being available for our sport. Only use them at suitable locations − and beware of causing annoyance to others.

Some owners replace their water box with a high-performance one. All the water

5 ADVANCED RIDING

WARNING

Some of the techniques and manoeuvres outlined in this chapter involve an element of risk. Neither the publishers of *The Jet Ski Book* nor the manufacturers of Kawasaki Jet Ski personal watercraft can accept liability for any consequences arising from readers' use or attempted use of these techniques.

DEVELOPING SKILLS

Once you gain confidence in your ability to control the Jet Ski you will probably want to try out some more advanced manoeuvres. There are a whole series of these, some developed specifically to get a racing Jet Ski round courses faster, others for their spectacle value. We'll look at both, with tips from the experts.

As always, take the manoeuvres step by step. Don't be too ambitious when you first start: some of these techniques can be dangerous if you don't have full control of the Ski.

TURNING

The first step towards advanced riding is to tighten up your turns. Corners of less than 75 degrees are fast: you can keep the throttle wide open if you set up properly and get the Ski on edge. Anything over 75 degrees and you'll have to approach it at three-quarters to full throttle. But from 90 degrees up-

Throwing your whole body in to carve tighter turns is effective, impressive and very tiring

wards it's a slow corner, for which you will have to develop a technique.

The tightest turn you are likely to have to make in racing is about 120 degrees: if it were 180 you'd be turning back into traffic and that would be dangerous. The one thing you can't do is back off the throttle before entry and then apply full power halfway round: as the water pressure in the pump eases, for a vital few seconds the impeller will be spinning in air and you will lose all drive.

RIGHT Using your legs as a brake. Stick it in hard to help you slow down and turn

BELOW It's not your speed into corners that matters — it's your speed out of them that will win you races

The 1985/86 world champion David Gordon says:

"What's important is the throttle control. A lot of riders just wrench it, but once the pump breaks loose, they're losing momentum. So get off the gas; it's much more important to keep 'fluid', keep the pump hooked up, than blip the throttle wide open, have the pump break loose, have the revs go through the ceiling. You'll be going nowhere quick...

"Slow down a little bit sooner than you might think, set up better, get the boat on edge, get 'sunk' into the turn real nice and power through it – that's the way to do a tight corner." The top riders' secret, he says, is not their high speed into the corner but their fast speed out.

"If you go into a corner too fast, you're going to lose time exiting. You can only go into a corner so fast. Coming out fast is a matter of how well you set up for it – especially on high-powered boats like modifieds.

"When you're approaching a slow corner, feather the throttle, set up, turn the handlebars. Sometimes you might want to come off the throttle completely. You'll slide for an instant and then slow down. The boat slows down very quickly when you come off the gas but, remember, you can't steer when you have no power.

"The next move is to get the Jet Ski on edge. Don't put the power back on until the Ski is pointing in the right direction. It also helps if you 'sweep' your turn. Don't make the mistake that a lot of riders make – they try to square off the corner by approaching it in a straight line, then making a very sharp turn. It's better to give the buoy some room going in and feather the throttle about 10ft from it, but don't throttle off completely. The Ski will slide for about five feet. About 3–5ft before the buoy, gas it and bring yourself around."

Leg drag turns

On smooth water you can use your leg as a brake. Go in hard to a corner and stick your leg in deep to brake at the last second. Pull your leg up again as soon as possible. You want to get back on the throttle right away and if you're dragging your leg too long you're wasting time.

British 1990 Champion Phil Wade recalls:

"I remember when I competed in my first event, which was now a few years ago. Jet Ski racing was still a relatively new sport to this country, and I recall that nearly every competitor had their own individual style of riding. Some riders were very creative, but there didn't seem to be any uniformity.

"Then, in 1988, a guy called John 'Cowboy' Cook came over from the States to compete in the full British and European Championships. For the first time, British riders saw how an American handled a Jet Ski. We'd all heard that the Americans were good, so as soon as Cowboy Cook started using his leg over the side of the Ski to help him turn, just about everyone else adopted the same style.

Although this method of turning is very effective, especially in long, sweeping corners, it can be very tiring. So, to use the technique throughout a race, you'll have to be very fit.

Step 1. Approach the corner in your normal riding position, choosing your line through the corner.

Step 2. As you get closer to the turn buoy, move your leg (left leg for right corners, right leg for left corners) towards the inside of the Ski nearest the turn.

Step 3. Your other leg – the one nearest the turn buoy – should now be on the outside of the Ski, enabling you to pull the Ski over and bank it into the turn.

Step 4. Pull the Ski over and let your lower leg skim across the top of the water.

This will act as a waterski. Now put your body weight onto your lower leg, allowing the Ski to carve the turn.

Step 5. Keep this position throughout the turn until you are facing in the right direction. Then ease your body weight off your lower leg.

Step 6. As the Ski straightens, bring your leg back inside the tray and adopt your normal riding position.

Some riders, on tight turns, throw their hip into the water and pull the Ski round. Again, this is tiring and you have to remember to keep your weight forward.

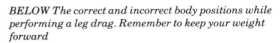

BELOW The correct and incorrect body positions while performing a leg drag. Remember to keep your weight forward

Wrong – leaning too far back

Right – correct body position

Wrong – leaning too far back

Right – correct body position

FREESTYLE

The best way to learn freestyle is to watch other freestylers. Watch them, learn the basic moves and then start trying your own variations. In competitive freestyling, variations and smooth transitions are the way to win, but before developing your own repertoire you need to learn the basic tricks outlined here.

Some of the best tricks were invented by accident. Top freestyler Scott Watkins says: "The first trick I learned started as an accident, a spin-out. I was out there riding hard, trying to make a hard turn, and just started spinning out – did a 180.

"Eventually, I mastered the spin-out. Those led (almost automatically since your momentum's going backward) into learning to do a tail stand. After you do enough tail stands, you discover tail spins, which are just a matter of going brrAPP-brrAPP-brrAPP, gently on the throttle, with the handlebar turned and one leg out. You start to spin round one way or the other.

"That's how it goes, one move leads you into another. When you've mastered all the basic moves, you can start thinking about variations and clean transitions from one move to another."

One-hand 180-degree slide

Step 1. Ride along at about half-throttle and start to lean to one side as if you were going to turn.

Step 2. Now quickly turn the bars and rev the throttle, which will cause the back end of the machine to break away and start sliding.

One-hand 180-degree slides. Go into a slide . . .

. . . and as the Ski starts to break loose, lift a hand off the handlebars

Step 3. As the Ski rotates through 180 degrees and starts to travel backwards, lift your hand off while trying to maintain your balance.

Step 4. As the Ski comes to a halt, replace your hand onto the bars and ride off.

You can also go into a one-handed tail spin from this manoeuvre or a 360-degree pirouette in the tray.

Spins

Step 1. Lean forward a little and turn sharply, hitting the gas.

Step 2. The forward lean gets the weight going towards the nose. When you spin, you pivot on the nose and the tail whips around. As soon as the back of the boat breaks away, ease off the throttle to prevent the machine overrevving.

Step 3. Your Jet Ski is now going backwards. When your momentum drops, you can either ride it out or lean back into a tail stand.

The key to spinning is getting the weight off the tail and letting the water squirting out of the jet pump spin you around. If you have too much weight on the back of the boat, your ride plate will dig in and you will stop hard and fast. Go as slowly as necessary. If you're going too fast you will just fly backwards out of control.

Controlled low-speed spins do require some extra low-end power. It's also easier if your Jet Ski has some type of quick-turn system such as a trick steer.

360-degree spin. Lean forward, turn sharply and hit the gas. As soon as the back of the Ski breaks away, ease off the throttle

Tail spin

Step 1. There are two ways to enter into a tail spin:

a) by slowing down, transferring your weight to the rear of the Ski, to force the rear underwater; or

b) by putting the Ski into a 180-degree slide, and while sliding backwards transferring your weight to the rear of the Ski. As the Ski begins to stop, the rear will again submerge under the water.

Step 2. With the rear of the machine under the water, drop one foot off the Ski, and let it trail in the water to act as a stabiliser. The other foot must be positioned at the back of the tray to keep the back submerged.

Step 3. Depending on which foot you have dropped, lean the Ski slightly to that side, turning the bars in that direction. With this combination apply a little throttle to keep the Ski vertical. The machine will now begin to rotate.

Step 4. With the Ski rotating you can now apply more throttle to increase rotation. Keep the circles as tight and as small as possible to make this manoeuvre more impressive.

Tail spin. Keep the circles as tight as possible to make this manoeuvre more impressive

360-degree nose spin

Step 1. Make a hard left or right turn, hard enough so that the nose starts to dig into the water. As you turn, keep the Ski banked over but your body fairly upright.

Step 2. As the pump comes out of the water hit the throttle on full lock. This will help to spin the back round.

Step 3. Throw all your weight and handlepole forward as you spin the Ski on its nose. It helps counterbalance the angle of the Ski if you lean outside the turn.

Keep the Ski on full lock through the turn and ride out. The more you practise this trick, the more spray you will get, and the more impressive the trick will be.

360-degree nose spin. The more you practise this trick the more spray you will kick up

360-degree pirouette

This is also referred to as a tray spin, but it is you, rather than the Ski, that does the spinning.

Step 1. Riding slowly, ease off the throttle, and throw the handlepole forward and up.

Step 2. Spin 360 degrees in the tray — not too fast, or you'll lose your balance.

Step 3. Catch the handlebars as they come down and ride on.

Fountain of youth

Step 1. Ride along on your knees at about half-throttle. Reach forward with your left hand and take hold of the air scoop.

Step 2. Now rotate your body through 180 degrees so you're facing backwards on the handlepole.

Step 3. Slow down to tickover to allow the front of the ski to sink under the water.

Step 4. As it sinks, apply throttle again and a large fountain should shoot out from the jet.

360-degree pirouette. Throw the handlepole up, spin round in the tray and catch it as it comes down

The fountain of youth. Reach forward, spin round, sink the Ski, then throttle up – and soak your friends!

One-hand, one-leg hood stand

Step 1. With the Ski travelling in a straight line, step forward with your left foot on to the centre of the hood.

Step 2. Stay in this position until you are comfortable, then extend your right leg out to the right.

Step 3. Once you are used to being in this position, remove your left arm and extend it out to the side.

This trick looks better if you keep the Ski steady and have your arms and legs very straight.

ABOVE One-hand, one-leg hood stand. Carefully step up onto the hood, then extend your right leg and left arm

Riding backwards

This basic trick is more difficult than it looks. The first thing to do is get used to operating the throttle with your left hand. You can practise this while you are riding along forwards.

Don't undertake this manoeuvre unless the water is completely clear of other traffic, and while you are riding backwards keep looking over your shoulder.

Step 1. Remove your left hand from the handlebars and transfer it to the throttle. Use your little finger on the throttle and put your middle finger between the lever and the grip – this stops you over-accelerating and making a fast exit.

Step 2. Let go with your right hand and start to turn your body in the tray.

Step 3. With your body turned through 180 degrees, place your right hand on the left grip. Now ease yourself upright and spread your feet. Increasing speed will improve your balance. Some riders find the trick easier and the boat more stable if they rest their backside against the handlepole pad.

Now try turning. Once you have mastered this trick, you can make it more impressive by stepping one foot at a time up to the rails, then on to the hood cover. Take each step slowly and maintain a steady throttle.

If you want to be still more flash you can stand on one leg on the hood with your right arm in the air. To do this move your right foot on to the hood cover strap. Shift all your weight to this leg, and move your left leg out to the side. Practise moving your left leg away from your body and bringing it back in before you proceed. The final flourish is to wave your right hand in the air.

ABOVE Riding backwards. The manoeuvre as it looks on the water

Grasp the throttle with your left hand and turn round slowly

Use the little finger on your left hand as a 'throttle limiter'

Resting on the handlepole pad may make the ski more stable

Barefoot backwards: sitting

This has nothing to do with whether you have shoes on or not, but is so called because of its similarities to barefoot waterskiing.

Step 1. From a kneeling position, lean forward and grasp the air intake with your left hand. Now pull yourself up onto the hood. Keep your weight up on top of the handlepole for ease of balance.

Step 2. Ride as fast as you can handle and slide down onto the front of the pole. Dig your feet into the water and skim along.

Step 3. Now lift up your free arm and look forward. This looks stylish and makes the trick a lot safer.

Barefoot backwards. Ride as fast as you can handle and plant your feet in the water. Lift one arm up and look forward. This makes the trick safer and more stylish. Once you have mastered it sitting down, try it standing – but make sure you are going fast enough to stand on the water. This trick can be dangerous if you fall

Barefoot backwards: standing

This freestyle manoeuvre produces a lot of spray, making it look very impressive.

The key to barefooting backwards on a Jet Ski is speed. You need to be going fast enough to allow you to stand on the water. But be careful not to ride into the bank while going backwards.

Step 1. Starting in a kneeling position at about half-throttle, lean forward and grip the air intake on the hood with your left hand. Now reverse your throttle hand so the lever is controlled with your thumb.

Step 2. Pulling with your left hand, rotate your body through 180 degrees on the pole.

Towards the end of the rotation switch hands, placing your left hand on the throttle and your right on the left grip. Having reached this position, proceed for a while getting the general feel of going backwards.

Step 3. When comfortable, increase throttle to about three-quarters and place the tips of your feet into the water towards the front of the Ski. With one quick movement place all your weight onto your feet and stand up, bringing the pole up with you between your legs.

One-foot barefoot

Step 1. Practise riding the Ski in a straight line at nearly full speed in a kneeling position.

Step 2. Leaning forward over the handlepole, keep the throttle open with the right hand and get hold of the air intake on the hood with your left hand.

One-foot barefoot

Swing over the side and dig your feet into the water. It helps if you keep your legs straight

Step 3. When you feel balanced with your body at a 45-degree angle across the Ski, swing your body and feet out to the left side of the Ski and, still keeping full throttle, straighten your legs out with your feet on the water. Sit on the handlebars.

Step 4. Practise this a few times, then when you feel comfortable with both feet on the water, try lifting one foot. It will feel very difficult at first and puts great strain on the stomach muscles and groin, but do persevere because this trick looks impressive once achieved.

When you are comfortable with both feet in the water, lift your left leg to make the trick more spectacular

How to hold the Ski for the one-foot barefoot trick

Bulldog

From the barefoot position it is easy to go into the bulldog, where you look as if you are wrestling with the Ski. Slow down, dig your feet in and turn the handlebars quickly into a left turn. The nose of the Ski will dig in, and the back slide around. Pull yourself up onto the handlepole and face the back of the Ski. Keep your upper body over the bars and accelerate away.

Side ride

Yet another variation on barefooting. Don't try it in rough water.

Step 1. Riding at full speed, put your left foot in the water and barefoot.

Step 2. Once you are used to the feel of the water and the feel of the Ski, lean forward, take your left hand off the handlebars and tuck the bars against your side.

Step 3. Pull on the bars with your right hand. This stops you from turning left and also keeps you upright.

LEFT Side ride. A simple way to get the feel for barefooting

Head stand. It's probably worth practising this on dry land first

Head stand

Step 1. Ride the Jet Ski in a kneeling position at about three-quarters throttle.

Step 2. Grasp the air intake with your left hand and swing around on to the handlepole. You will now be facing backwards. Quickly grasp the throttle with your left hand and accelerate.

Step 3. Decelerate slightly and slide down, putting your head in the tray.

Step 4. Pull your legs up into a head stand position.

Step 5. Accelerate so the air pressure helps keep you upright.

From this position you can make the trick more impressive by doing the scissors, i.e. parting your legs and bringing them together again. Don't hold the head stand for more than a few seconds, because you can't see where you are going and you are likely to have lost your sense of direction.

180-degree nose stab

This is also called the Bucking Bronco. Once mastered, it is one of the most impressive manoeuvres around. You'll probably have a few duckings while learning it, but that's part of the fun of freestyle.

Step 1. Bounce the Ski up and down, so that it begins to leave the water with each bounce.

Step 2. After one or two bounces, when you have reached a reasonable height, push really hard on the next bounce and gas the throttle.

Step 3. As the Ski begins to leave the water, fully turn the bars. This will give the back end a kick and it will begin to rotate in the air.

Step 4. With the back end moving, push the nose downwards so that as the Ski lands the nose submerges.

Step 5. Keep the bars turned; the Ski will turn under water and then surface again.

OPPOSITE & BELOW *The 180-degree nose stab. One of the most impressive tricks. Bounce the Ski to get some height, then push hard on the next bounce, gas the throttle, turn the bars as the Ski leaves the water, then push the nose down*

Submarine

Step 1. Ride at about half-throttle and look for calm, deep water. Bounce your Ski several times, then point the nose downward.

Step 2. Apply pressure to the sides of the tray with your ankles. This will help to pull the pump out of the water as you push the nose forward and down.

Step 3. As the nose goes in, get your weight back, arms outstretched and head down. Make sure you dive in straight: if not you will be pulled off the Ski by the force of the water. As you go down, tuck your head down and streamline your body. Don't apply too much throttle underwater unless you want a hull-full.

Step 4. Pull yourself upright and lean back to pull yourself and the Ski out of the submarine.

*Submarine. Make sure the water is deep enough before
you try this spectacular trick*

SEA AND SURF

There's nothing to stop a beginner taking to the sea in calm conditions. As your handling of the Ski improves, you can go further out in progressively steeper waves and really begin to make the most of the craft.

For extensive sea use, you may need a couple of modifications: the bilge pump mentioned in Chapter 4, and also perhaps a larger fuel tank. The standard tank takes 13 litres – about two hour's worth, or 35 miles in the sea. A 22-litre tank could therefore be a good investment for sea riders. The nose will seem heavy when you start, but that's only to be expected when you have nearly twice as much fuel on board. Large fuel tanks have to be filled in the engine bay, not through the normal fuel filler.

Since Jet Ski watercraft are not designed for wave jumping, it might also pay to strengthen the hull by reinforcing the front near all seams and edges, then pulling out the fuel tank, removing all of the green glue in the nose cone and sticking down four sheets of 7oz glassfibre with epoxy resin.

A couple of tips for sea skiing. Ride early or late. It's probably best to ride before 10am and after 5pm. There are two reasons for this. Firstly, you're more likely to have the water to yourself and, secondly, it gets choppier in the middle of the day. As the sun heats up the land, the warm air rises and cold air rushes in to fill the space. The result is a fresh onshore wind.

When jumping, you should always be aware of the wind direction before you leave shore. Try to jump into the wind: cross-winds can easily blow you sideways and cause you to lose control in mid-air.

Finally, be aware of your surroundings. Watch out for other water users and for strange patterns in the water – it could signal a shallow area or rocks.

Wave-jumping is great fun – but since Jet Skis are not designed for landing from big waves it might be an idea to strengthen the hull and nose cone if you intend doing it a lot

Wave jumping

One of the world's best freestylers is Scott Watkins. "Taking off on a jump is easy," he says. "Landing is the tricky part. Even so, the take-off is critical because it determines how you will land. The motion you get on the wave is amplified when you are in the air. If you rev it on take-off the nose will continue at the angle of the wave. If you let off right at the crest the nose will roll forward in the air, and you come down nose first. If this happens, squat down and tuck in when you hit the water. If you stay standing you'll hit the water like a door.

"Ideally, you want to land at a 45-degree angle, with the pump in the water. Also, this angle is best for soaking up the jolt when you hit the water. The boat knifes in, and the angle deflects through your legs. The worst thing is to land flat – you'll get pounded.

"One thing to remember is that anytime the pump is out of the water the throttle is off. Don't rev it in the air. Hit the throttle the second the pump is in. If you're out of shape when you land, you can usually pull it out with the throttle.

"It's hard to make mid-air corrections on a Jet Ski because you can't use the throttle to change the angle of the boat. This gets back to the take-off part. If the nose is too high when you are in the air there isn't much you can do – pushing on the bars has little effect.

"If the nose is too low, try pushing down with your legs to get the tray lower. The nose should come up.

"Study the waves to figure out the patterns, stay centred and balanced, get the angle you want on take-off so the boat goes in the air at the right attitude, keep the nose up, soak up the landing with your legs, and gas it the second you're in."

180-degree turns

If you want to get flashy, doing a 180 in the air is the trick. Here's how Scott Watkins does it:

"As you hit the face of the wave, lean forward a little more than normal. This helps get the nose to start down. As you reach the crest, turn the bars all the way to one side, usually left, and rev hard. Remember that whatever motion you set up in the water is amplified in the air. As the tail comes around, keep leaning forward, but push out against the tray with your outside foot. This helps control the turn in the air.

"Keep your arms flexed so you can push out to get the nose down. If they are straight you won't have much control.

"You want the nose to penetrate the water first. Don't land flat. Just relax, soak up the impact with your legs, and get on the gas the second the pump gets in the water.

"This is a tough trick to learn. The hard part is getting the nose down. When you first start, you will land flat most of the time. You have to use a lot of force to get the boat turned and the nose pushed down. It takes some muscle to make it happen, and lots of practice."

Surfing

Surfing provides one of the greatest thrills you can get on a Jet Ski. But don't overdo it: start in small surf and get the feel of the sea. Make sure your boat is in perfect shape mechanically – and, as always, have respect for other water users.

Scott Watkins again: "Catching the waves on a Jet Ski is pretty easy. If you're out of position a little you can just gas it – you don't have to paddle.

"Again you have to watch the waves, try to figure where they are going to start the break. If the water is shallow, the wave might be a little steeper. Keep the boat at an angle to the wave. Jet Skis don't work real well going straight down a wave – the back starts to jack up on you.

"Stay out in front of the wave towards the flat. A Jet Ski weighs about 300lb and it won't stay up in the curl. You can cheat it a little by keeping on edge in the wave and being smooth with the throttle. I like to lean into the wave just a little. If you catch an outside edge you're going to flip over, so I keep that inside edge cutting. I keep my feet centred and watch the water. "If the water is foaming or choppy, work back to smoother water so you can keep the pump driving. And watch for the wave clos-

ing out, try to get back out before you get stuck in the chop.

"A lot of good Jet Ski riders try to gas it when they get in trouble. Sometimes it works, sometimes it's better to let off for a second and drop back to smoother water. This is where surfing experience and knowing about the water comes into play. You have to work at getting a feel for the waves."

Depending on how rough the water is, Scott usually turns off the idle that makes the Jet Ski circle back if you fall off. "If you lose the craft, often it will end up 20 or 30 feet away, and if it's calm you can swim over. A small wave might push it over some

more, but no big deal. If the waves are big, it's going to flip over. If it stays running upside down the motor compartment is going to fill up through the intakes. Then you're in trouble. If the motor isn't idling it will just float upside down. Better to swim in and get it than have to drag it up with a winch. Decide what works for you.

"If it turns over, get on the side and pull it back up using your body to counterweight it. Before you try to start, hit the bilge pump and be sure the motor compartment is empty. Then hit the starter button."

6 RACING

COMPETITION

By the time you have a good grasp of the advanced techniques introduced in the last chapter you may be thinking about pitting your skills against those of others. Like most sports, Jet Ski racing is becoming increasingly sophisticated, but it's still new enough to give relatively inexperienced riders with standard or near-standard machines a run for their money. Here we offer a few tips.

Every year more women are getting out on the race course – and winning

Jet Ski racing demands a high level of fitness. If you ski regularly, it'll keep you fit, but if you can't ski as often as you like, or if you stop for the winter, you'll need to keep your muscle tone up with a good series of muscle-strengthening exercises such as weight lifting. Arms, chest, back, stomach and legs all need attention. Regular bouts of squash, cycling, swimming or other sports will also help.

GETTING OFF TO A GOOD START

In closed-course racing, above all else you need to be able to make a good start. The top riders are difficult to overtake, so you have to get in front of them from the off. Being the first rider to the first buoy gives you a distinct advantage. It means, first, that you have much smoother water; and, secondly, that the others have to worry about overtaking you – which won't be easy. It's far easier to stay in front of someone than to pass them.

A lot of races are won or lost by a rider's performance on the startline. In any competition, tension is at its highest at the start, so it is important to get your mind focused on the job in hand well in advance. Avoid other distractions.

It helps if you are prepared for your race well ahead of the start time. This means having your lifejacket and spinal protection, racing number and helmet at the ready, and your Jet Ski fuelled up with the engine warm. Nothing is more unnerving than to be called for your race, only to find that your helmet straps are tangled or your race number is in the kitbag in the changing room. Having prepared yourself for the start, line up in good time.

Different clubs require different starts – shallow-water, deep-water, jetty and so on

– but the most common seems to be the shallow-water start.

Gone are the days when the race director would wave a flag to signal the start of a race. By then the majority of machines had already left the startline, so unless you were equally good at jumping the start, or very lucky, you didn't stand a chance.

Now, at the majority of clubs, starts are much more sophisticated, with mechanical starting gates bringing about a much-needed improvement. You draw a number

LEFT The start is probably the most important part of the race

denoting your own position on the startline. Once in position, try to get a good foothold, especially on gravel: not only will it help you to hold the Ski prior to the start, but it will also ensure you keep your footing when the thrust comes on. It's also important to have a holder that you can trust to help hold the Ski steady and in position.

The start gate official will tell everyone to start their engines. The starter will hold up a 2-minute board. Anyone with an engine problem will now be given a maximum of two minutes to rectify it. After the two minutes are up – or immediately, if all engines are firing satisfactorily – the starter will raise the 1-minute board. The race can then go ahead.

Your holder stands on the opposite side of the Ski to you, preferably the air scoop side, since the scoop makes a good hand-hold. He should be close enough to you to be heard over the noise of the engines, since

ABOVE At the start, the holder should be close enough to hear you above the engine's roar

The holder needs to get a good grip on your machine

Pulling the Jet Ski out of the water and revving it to get rid of any excess water is one way of gaining a little extra speed off the mark

you will want him to tell you how far you can increase the revs before he finds it difficult to hold the Ski.

As the 1-minute board is laid on its side, make sure the handlebars are straight. Concentrate on watching the gate. As soon as it disappears, hit the throttle, bring your rear leg up into the tray and get it as near to the bulkhead as possible. Pull all of your upper body up and over the handlepole: this will automatically pull in your other

leg, and your head may actually touch the handlepole about halfway down.

It is important to get as much weight as possible onto the front of the Ski, which will make it plane quicker and stop it porpoising. Don't be in a hurry to stand up – wait until you get balanced and the Ski is stable and on the plane. If you stand too early, again the Ski may porpoise.

Practising a race start on your own

Make sure the handlebars are straight . . .

hit the throttle . . .

. . . and haul yourself aboard

The start is a tense moment, and should you jump or go through the elastic the race director will order a restart, making sure that this time you have a dead engine start and your throttle hand is way above your head!

Offshore pro Chris Fishetti says: "Pull the Jet Ski out of the water and rev it up to clear it out so you have no excess water or fumes in the boat. Then set it down in the water and hold it at a good rpm range. Come out of the hole smooth and straight. Pull the trigger and let the boat go. Stand up as soon as you can."

Overtaking

Having made a clean getaway, the next step is to cope with the rough water left by the rider in front of you. Every racer knows how difficult it is just to follow other riders in the rough water, but if you study the water carefully there are some smooth patches in the wake, just off centre, which can be used quite effectively to follow the rider in front until you sense an opportunity to overtake.

If you try following in a straight line down the middle of the wake, the chances are the Ski will be swayed from side to side by the turbulence and you will never get close enough to overtake. If you cannot find any smooth patches, try moving across the central part of the wake regularly to keep your balance.

In a race, the person in front of you will nearly always take the most direct route from marker to marker. This is not necessarily the fastest line for the corners, but it has the effect of blocking the corner for the rider behind. This in turn tends to slow the pace of the race and allows the leaders to get away. You therefore need to get by a blocker as quickly as possible. If the person in front leaves a gap between him and the marker, dive into it and take the corner.

Alternatively, study the course and find a tight section that leads onto a fast open stretch. Keep close to the rider in front and try crossing his wake as you take the corner. Take a wider line than him, and make a gradual loop to the next corner. If the rider in front has been watching you on the inside turn after turn, the sudden switch to the outside may be sufficient to allow you to take the next corner by surprise.

There are no hard and fast rules for overtaking, but we recommend practising it. Four-times world champion Jeff Jacobs trains with good riders and after accelerating away from them joins the back of the pack and practises working his way to the front again. Larry Rippenkroeger says: "If you're behind someone, pressure them and hope they make a mistake." Being fit will help as well. If you are going as strong on lap eight as you were on lap one, you will pass a lot of riders who are getting tired.

ABOVE The person in front enjoys a much smoother ride than the person behind

ABOVE & BELOW Sometimes you will be able to overtake on the inside . . .

. . . but usually you will have to go wide to pass the person in front BELOW

SLALOM

Slalom is all about precision and practice . . . and then more practice. It's you against five buoys and the clock. Jeff Jacobs says you should practise "an hour or two a day, two days a week". Practising like this, ideally on your own slalom course, not only makes you faster but also enables you to develop better lines around the buoys, making your performance more consistent.

The world champion also offers this advice: "I always try to keep my mind relaxed and positive, picturing myself doing a flawless run.

"Approaching the starting gate, I try to keep my boat lined up with the first buoy on the track and hold a relatively moderate speed so I don't overshoot it.

"Once through the gate, I really concentrate on my form and, more importantly, 'timing' the corners, turning exactly at the right location before each buoy, doing nothing that will result in a missed buoy or a wide turn.

"Since every rider has his or her own unique riding style, it's difficult to say how each corner should be taken. Besides, that's what practice is all about. There are, however, a few useful tricks: at the turnaround buoy, I come in wide so I can sweep it and the next buoy in one smooth, wide-open turn, one long motion.

"Since slalom is a timed event, don't concentrate so much on beating your competition. Instead, concentrate on beating the clock. Avoid porpoising in and out of the water, and try to stay hooked up all the

time. Keep your forward momentum up at all times and keep your turns tight.

"One last trick to keep in mind: on the World Tour, slalom consists of two runs and only the fastest run counts. On your first run, concentrate on being safe, smooth and fast so on your second run you can afford to go all out, going as fast as possible. If you mess up the second run, you can then fall back on your first one, but if you have a no-mistake second run, you'll have an amazing time on your hands."

You don't need a super-fast Ski for slalom. Slalom is not a question of who's got the fastest boat, more who is the smoothest rider. Compare the water behind the top riders and the rest. Jeff Jacobs is so smooth that the water behind him is almost calm. He glides into each buoy, while others

are sending up spray that will get in their way on the way back.

It's no coincidence that the winners in slalom are also usually the closed-course champions. You can practise closed-course until you're blue in the face, and still never be any good at slalom. But if you practise slalom you will find yourself doing a whole lot better in the closed course.

OPPOSITE & BELOW Slalom is a race against the clock. Remember to keep it smooth

RACING CLASSES

Jet Ski racing is organised into 11 closed-course and four slalom classes, enabling virtually any craft, from standard ex-factory models to fully-modified speed machines, to compete with Skis of similar performance. Although administered by national Jet Ski Associations, in the interests of standardising Jet Ski competition worldwide the regulations vary little between one country and another.

In closed-course competition, almost half the classes are novice classes: 300/440/550 Stock, 300/440 Superstock, 550 and 650 Limited and Modified. This allows you to try out the lower levels without spending a fortune on your machine, and if you are successful work your way up to the higher-powered classes.

In slalom, where raw power is less important than rider skill, all four classes will accept any level of Ski from Stock to Modified.

LEFT Typical fast-flowing Jet Ski action, seen at the 1990 Jet Ski British Open Championships . . .
. . . and on the warmer waters of the Pacific off the coast of California ABOVE

ABOVE Phil Wade taking the finals of the British Jet Ski Championships by storm

RIGHT World champion Jeff Jacobs

APPENDIX **USEFUL ADDRESSES**

International Jet Ski Boating Association
1239 E. Warner Avenue
Santa Ana
CA 92705
USA

Jet Ski International
Brinkworth House
Brinkworth
Chippenham
Wiltshire
SN15 5DF
United Kingdom

Kawasaki Information Service
7 Linford Forum
Rockingham Drive
Linford Wood
Milton Keynes
MK 14 6LY
United Kingdom

Kawasaki Jet Ski Europe NV
PO Box 532
2130 AM Hoofddorp
Amsterdam
The Netherlands

Kawasaki Motors Corporation USA
PO Box 25252
Santa Ana
CA 92799
USA

Kawasaki Motors (UK) Ltd
1 Dukes Meadow
Millboard Lane
Bourne End
Buckinghamshire
SL8 5XF
United Kingdom

UK Jet Ski Association
Goodwood Road
Boyatt Road Industrial Estate
Eastleigh
Hampshire
SO5 4NT
United Kingdom

EUROPE'S TOP JET SKI MAGAZINE

WE'RE WET & WILD

that's official!

JET SKI INTERNATIONAL

is the official magazine of the UK Jet Ski Association and is **FREE** to members

JET SKI INTERNATIONAL

is the only magazine aimed exclusively at the Jet Ski rider, with up-to-the minute coverage on training, tips, fashion, race reports, news and interviews with the stars. Whether you're a beginner or expert, there's no other choice for the best coverage on **YOUR** sport

FREE

WITH

EUROPE'S LEADING WATERSKI MAGAZINE

WATERSKI

INTERNATIONAL

ROAR INTO ACTION
WITH THE BEST

JET SKI